One 'n Done #7

Showboi
Too Deep Too Care

Poems by
Jimmy Cullen

Published by

ISBN: ISBN: 979-8-9868097-6-2

Library of Congress Control Number: 2023933263

Poetry

Memoir

Mental Health

LGBTQIA+

This is a work of fiction. Names, characters, business, events and incidents are the products of the author's imagination. Any resemblance to actual persons, living or dead, or actual events is purely coincidental.

For more information on *Showboi: Too Deep Too Care* or Read Furiously, please visit readfuriously.com. For inquiries, please contact info@readfuriously.com.

Read: [*v*] The act of interpreting and understanding language, symbols, and the written word.

Furiously: [*adv*] To do something with excitement and passion.

Read Often. Read Well.
Read Furiously

Prologue

The Legend of

Beyond the garden
There is a shelter
A haven
For all broken souls to heal

Inside the cottage
Is a magic man
With a magic chair
If you sit in it
Your world can change
For the better

I sat in this chair
In disbelief
Never believing in its magic
The power to elevate my soul
To rid it all of negative energies
Its power goes beyond comprehension
My mind
My heart
Changed

Beyond the garden
There is a haven
Where my soul heals
My mind breathes
My heart opens

The garden may be fading
But other avenues have opened
To protect my heart
Nurture my soul
To feel complete
When all seems lost

Wind Me Up (Hollow Heart)

You place the key in my lock
You twist it and there I go
Fulfilling all your dreams
Everything you expected of me

But when it stops what happens
All you see is a shell of a man
Dead eyes
And a hollow heart

Do I want you to put the key in my lock again
I don't think so
I can't live someone else's dreams
Dreams that aren't my own
I know what you expect of me

So it's your choice
I can't reach the lock
Do I continue to play out your dreams of me
Or wait to see what I do on my own

The Garden is Fading

This will be my life until I die
I cannot run
I cannot hide
From the burdening truth

I can run into the corners of my mind
Recline on a bed of soft roses
Come up with fantastic prose
But reality is sinking in

Run run
Take flight
Majestically soaring into the night sky
Make love with the stars

With every sunrise
Hope dwindles in my heart
Filled with empty promises
With a void growing larger each day

Act 1

The Story

I can hear the thunder
In the distance
Dark clouds rolling in
Leaving me isolated
In a garden of hellish delight
Colors drain from all the flowers
The sky turns blue to black
The sun fades
The moon shines
What I'm about to discover
Is beyond comprehension
The story of my life
Found in these
My words

A Well Worn Path

I arrive at the party late
I'm hidden behind a mask
No one can see what they don't

Doors open to a crowd of familiar faces
There is no hand to hold as I begin my procession
Faces smile and people cheer
Underneath I can shed no tears

I've walked this walk before
A path so weathered
It looks as if it's fading in time
When will this journey end
And my happiness begin

Bittersweet Roses

Moonlight
Illuminates my face
Glorifies my tears
Streaks of silver
Cascading down my face

In the night sky
There is a scent of a bonfire in the distance
It is welcomed
I am not
My fall from grace

The garden is not overgrown
I am
The garden is protection
It isn't anymore

It's time for me to evolve
To move along to another haven
This place once safe
Once called home
I've outgrown

The Demon Within

I feed on it
I crave your pain
Whenever you scream
I can match it with the hunger
That dwells within

No end in sight
I -
Your only option
To end what you call
Agony

By prolonging your anguish
I writhe in ecstasy
Almost erotic -
But not quite

You see
I've made a pact
An unforgivable one
In anger

Your screams
Were mine
Your freedom
I was once

What you will not understand
Is that like you
I have no escape

Agony and Ecstasy

Diamonds shimmy
When he walks down the marbled steps
No imperfections
Luminous

He enters the ballroom
Alone – no hand to hold
No one to call his own
They all bow
Divinity is present

Passing through oceans of warm pathetic bodies
He sets his sights on a worthy destination
He's not the one he's waited for -
Destined for
But he'll do

With one smile
He falls
Only a substitution for the real thing
Soon his smile fades

See Me Now

Physical tough
I cannot have
For I am otherworldly
A shadow
In your world of color

I exist in existence
Beyond physicality
Chained to this spot
For eternity

The blame is not yours
Although my actions say otherwise
But what can I do
This pact was made in both worlds
I can only blame me

A Son's Love

Lying in the dark
Knowing that it has come to an end
The TV illuminates my stoicism

Again I will rise from the pit
Again I will not surrender to crippling anxieties
I will not allow this to hinder my duty
My honor
My love
To take care of one who has given life to me
There will be no moment when I will abandon her
Even if I shall find someone
My pledge will not go undone

Lying here in illumination, I will let the anxieties take
over just one last time
For sleep is heaven
I fear I won't see it

A World Without You

I run to my garden
In tears
To the roses
Of which have not overgrown
I have not tended to them in years

Caressing the smooth petals
I recount all that has come my way
Successes
Failures
Losses

I can't understand why he had to go
As I ruminate on this thought, continuously
I tear a petal off a single rose
With each tear
I feel a stabbing pain in my heart

I cannot feel the thorns
Pressing deeply into my palm
As I strangle the poor flower
Trying to make sense of this chaos

The flower is bald

My hand is bloody

My face is wet

Can we live in a world without him

Darkest Night

Empty words and hallow prayers
These are difficult times
When my mind keeps rolling
Constantly taunting me
With false truths
Fake smiles

What could I ask God for now
Daddy's dead
I am still here
God's will is purposeful
And exact

I must continue on
Whether it be through times of grief
Or when I want to slit my own throat
I must close my eyes now
And hopefully wake up in a world unshattered

I Wish, I Wish

I wish my mouth was sewn shut
To keep inside all the bad from coming out
Let my body speak instead
With all the voices it houses
Screams, shrieks, moans, groans
You'll never know who you're speaking to

I wish my vocal chords were cut
To keep them from drowning me in a world of hate
Let my eyes vocalize the pain I have inside
Too little to satiate
How little you know about me – surprising

I wish I were blind so I could not see
All the hate
All of the world I wish to leave behind
But what then
Inside I'd be stuck with images of unwanted mem-
ories
Malicious imagery
For the rest of my life
There would be no peace

Is that what it wants

Sometimes I wish I were dead
To leave behind these ideas and thoughts plaguing
my mind like clockwork
Whenever it appears
It sinks in its talons
Digging its fangs into my jugular

I wish for the pain to go away
I wish for me to go away, one day

Never Pleased

What can I do
I'm the penultimate showgirl
Everyone's mascot
I bring smiles to hundreds of people
But never to myself

What can be missed
In an empty shell of a life
Secluded from the public
Only the farce can be seen
To make sure I keep things moving

Why must I keep moving
To continue on this path so worn
No one to share it with
I can hope all I want
They can keep lying to me
But I feel the outcome is as depressing as I know it
will be

Ring Bell For Service

Have you ever been abandoned
Can you say you've been alone
Walked this earth with no hand to hold
Felt a presence so strong that you've grabbed hold
Only to be left alone
Again

My body is like a grand hotel
There is always a vacancy in the presidential suite
Many a person have occupied it
Our most infamous guest "Ego" or "It"
Has occupied that suite many a times

Like a house of cards
I fold easily
There is no one but myself to pick up the pieces
What I've learned so far is
There were no inhabitants
Just vacancies

I thought I was the vigilant,
Permanent resident of my body

This grand hotel

Shockingly, I am not a permanent resident

I vacate the premises more often than not

What I leave behind is a shell

A structure that eats

Thinks sometimes, never sleeps

Constantly waiting for the next guest to check in

Who will it be

Act 2

The Wallflower Life

Everyone was gay
All was bright
No tears
All cheers

For every suit
There was a rose
For every wrist
A corsage

Men and women danced with each other
Celebrating love and life
To every pot there was a lid

I, the wallflower,
Dwelled in the shadows
Awaiting my invitation
It never came

An empty vessel, I am
Always heartbroken
Surrounded by such joy
Drowned in so many tears

A Mute's Frustrations

It's slowly hitting me
You've been here all my life
Now you have taken a final bow

What you gave us was sensational
We are all grateful
For you wisdom
Insights
They never proved wrong

None of us could've imagined
What was bound to happen
Then it happened

Lying in bed
I can only wonder when
I can feel again
Being emotionally mute
Keeps me together

My heart is shattered
By the absence of you

Of your son, my father

Right now it feels like
I will never be able to feel again
To really be human

Trying To Understand This World Without You

I know you are there now
I miss you already
You know I am unique in my feelings
I don't express them too much
Don't wish to burden others
I just want to be private

Struggling to feel any emotion after your death was
exhausting
I was filled with memories that kept me warm
Cheered me up
However, there was no sign of present emotion

What do you expect
I lost my father so suddenly
I tried to end my life so early
All because I felt too much and no one seemed to
care

You cared
You cared so deeply about my well-being

You knew I had that light
You knew I would carry on as expected

No longer do I mourn
I only celebrate what we had together
A love with a bond so strong
A friendship I will cherish forever

Muriel's Prayer

Never knew my heart could beat so steadily
I can laugh, work, and eat
Only in bed
I wonder where is the emotion
How come there are no tears

You must know I loved you deeply
Holding on to every memory
All those funny moments
Never to forget what you taught me

To be myself
Be kind to others
Find understanding in life

I will never forget you
My heart will hold on tight
I hope you are at peace

The Wrong Way

I should be used to it by now
The unsettling
Sinking feeling
There's something in the air

I know what's supposed to happen
It's been done my whole life
Why can't it just stay the same
Life is unfair, cruel
That's evident

As I start to separate
Like gum stuck to a shoe
I slowly expand, stretching
Separating my body from my mind

At one point
I reside only in my mind
Looking through my eyes
Watching what he does
What he doesn't do

So come with me
Into a separate space
And watch my life go by
Unable to stop the unspeakable
Watching someone live my life
The wrong way

Fine China

Why did I fall
I reached out to you
You weren't there

When I hit the ground
My shattering is what alerted you
Finally you come running
Rushing to find me broken into a billion pieces
Only then do you reach out to me

Hoping to reconstruct my body
The fortress that keeps you alive
A place where it's empty inside
Barren
Void of love
The only thing that's clear is fact that no one could
possibly love me

I am needed
When needed
And can only be reached
When I'm at my worst

Just So You Know

My time is drawing near
How I hate myself for what I put myself through
Never knowing who's pushing or shoving
When the boat gets rocked
There's no captain in sight

Why should it matter how I feel or what I do
Life seems so pointless
Losing him dimmed my shine
I know that now
I loved him

Like a sovereign with their duties
I have a duty to my family
I must keep my head out of the fire
Retain composure
And slip slowly back into the role of
The ugly duckling

We All Have Monsters

Right now my mind is tired

My body wishes to rest

But you continue to irk me

Pushing me aside

In order to seek dominance

Power over my physical body

To feel free again

To destroy all I've created

What can be done

To something that is natural

For something that I'll experience till death

I just pray for it to be brief

For my absence to be minor

Hoping no one will notice

A Perishing Paradise

Lush vegetation
Why would I ever want to leave
Lightning cracks
The sun takes its bow
Leaving me in the garden
In the dark
Flowers perishing

I pick myself up and run for cover
The storm is playful
Giving me time to seek refuge
I know what seeks me
It can't hide its ferocity

Passing fountains
Perishing vegetation
I approach my prison
The golden palace

I've accepted the inevitability
I'll have to play the game
Do the dance
I must keep them all happy
When I'm unhappy

Awkward

Quick glance
I don't want to be noticed
I'm not trying to make conversation
Please don't recognize me

I vaguely remember you
What is there to know more about
Than what's posted on Facebook
I still want that veil
The divider

I don't want to seem rude
Or in complete ignorance
Of your existence
I just want to remain unrecognizable

I guess I'm still socially awkward
Since his death
I'll continue to hide behind that veil
Until someone makes me take it down

Leave Me Be

I wish to sleep soundly
Not wanting to think too deeply
I feel too deeply
I get so addicted to the chemical change
What is natural for me is unforgivable to others

He's so alluring
The glow
Illuminating his body
Promises me salvation
Shelter from the disease
He is the disease

I may be standing still
But I'm running from him
The more I resist
The closer he gets
I've gotten stronger
And so has he

I cannot outrun him
He is me – invincible, immortal

Suddenly I stop
A smile appears on my face
It isn't mine

What Happens Next

As the sun goes down
On another day
I count my blessings

As the moon shines
And the clouds disappear
Everything becomes so queer

Am I tired or exhausted
Of living in a world without you
How does time move forward now

At night I clear my mind
Go over all the parts of the day
Realizing something's gone awry

The time has come for me
To rest my head on my pillow
Pray harder than before
Hoping the pain won't last

Lolito (The One They Love To Hate)

You can't be around people
When I appear
Slowly I pour hot cement into your veins

You'll never know when I'm ready
To seize all control over your being
Pushing you aside
Out of the picture
Out of focus
Out of mind

I have been with him since childhood
On that day he ended up in that driveway
Crying over a boy
He didn't even want

I am Lolito
The boy who knows all of your buttons
Who pulls the wool over your eyes
When the one you love wishes to flee

Sit back and enjoy the show you all love to hate

The personality of many

That hides the one you treasure most

Jekyll Meet Hyde

I can say hello and goodbye
All at once
Without hesitation

It's like a kaleidoscope
With each turn something new appears
Whether or not it's willing to

Suppressed pain
Memories best kept hidden
I succumb to the pressures of him

I try to maintain control but at what cost
I can say hello and goodbye simultaneously
You'll never know who's standing before you
A shadow
Or burst of energy, a wave of dangerous light

Intermission

A Torrid Affair

Hungrier than ever
I can eat everything in sight
If I wanted to

These days pop out of nowhere
Catching me off guard
Covering my eyes with a film
My head with a veil
Which strangles me now

I don't know who will come out
Always a mystery
He doesn't seem to save me
But to ruin all that I built
To close me off to the world
Protecting me from any emotions

Fingers numb
Kisses cold
I'll let this personality take hold

Reflection

Sometimes I'm so disconnected from my words
Always realizing they capture a brief moment in time
of what I feel
What I experience
Whether it be mania or grief
I find myself empowered by these words
Words that capture my mind
The waves of emotions
The crippling side effects of mania

Sometimes I don't want to write
Experience life without examination
Mostly I don't want to initiate another war
All I can say is I'm getting better
Not cured
Just better at dealing with these experiences I docu-
ment

For now I sign off
Letting my mind take rest
Letting the muscles of the mind rebuild
Getting stronger with each upset

The Intrigue

An unknown sensation
Pleased to see you
You are pleased to see me
What's good for you
Is a mystery to me
I have no radar

Bewildered
Beguiled
By the mystery that is you
The feelings you awake in me
It seems endless
Always an ongoing dialogue
With no closure

Human, Again

Suddenly
I am surrounded by many lights
Different colors
Different shapes
And sizes

All familiar to me
What was so distant
Is now so clear
They were with me all the time

I dance in circles
Giggling
My age retrograding
Hoping our tango never stops

What was once dark
Is light
Without these illuminations
How could my soul
Have sight

Act 3

The Gift

Somewhere deep inside
She's happy with his delivery
Silently smiling beneath her stone facade
Missing her beloved
Happily, she knows he's her gift

This is a message from Daddy
From God himself
Showing that her work isn't done
Her life isn't empty without him
She has her family, and grandson
A son and a daughter who still need her
Like they need their father

A parental presence is always needed
Wisdom, stability, love
To give up now
To say goodbye to the gift your husband gave to you
Would be a waste

As I said to Daddy before he passed

"You are needed"

"You are wanted"

"You are loved"

"Please stay with us"

Dangerous

When the well runs dry
Tears aren't any use to you anymore
You've entered into a state of mind most dangerous

Saying goodbye seems not as important as before
Not knowing if you're letting go for good
Or just floating through time
Filled with emptiness and no emotion

These are dangerous times
All you can do is hope
Hope that the end to the void is nearer
Than the act of pure selfishness

Custody Battle

You moved me in ways no one has known
You've brought me down to my knees
Wanting to claw my eyes out
Tear at my heart
Bare all my sins
Leading me to one alternative

Right now I'm residing in my body
I'm the master of this ship
No longer will you bring me to my knees
I'll continue on this journey
Not blindly

I know you will return
I know I will leave
I've never wanted to exist so much
It hurts

To Alleviate Your Pain

It hurts you that it hurts me
When I leave my body
When no emotion or sensitivity is present
Leaving behind a corpse
Strung up like a puppet
An asylum patient
Being fed pills hoping to cure the incurable
To satiate the unfamiliarity
The uneasiness that comes with loneliness
I'm sorry to hurt you
I'm sorry I can't decide when these processes will
begin
I shall speak of this pain no longer
I shall be silent
Draw a smile on my face
Act like everything will pass
When in reality it will choose its end

Restoril Affair

I wish I could have more of you

Drown in your divine

Swim in an ocean full of you

How many times have I thought about it

How many times I decided against it

Your love is stronger

Your comfort rejuvenates me

If it wasn't for my past

I'd never met you

Without that overdose

I'd never know such bliss

What Tomorrow Brings

My emotions are starting to shift again
Nothing celebratory
For we know what the shifts bring

I can hear him inside
Radiating light
Giving me hope

He is somewhere in there
Behind the ivy
Through the fog
Somewhere in the garden
Waiting to regain prominence

For now I remain empty
Bracing myself for this shift
It's what I'm used to
What does that mean to you

Personal Hell

Your worries mean nothing to me
For my body is void of all emotions
The light within my eyes dull
I can't concentrate on anything
Try my best to bring myself out of it
But there is no point
This poison fills my veins
Swallows my light
When the tantrum is over it will be relinquished

I try my hardest to be there for my mother
But the silence is deafening
Leaving both of us isolated
Lost in our own personal hells

I know this moment will pass
But its staying power is unknown
A day, a week, maybe a year
Nothing compares to that one year
When I said goodbye

Sometimes I think about overdosing
Swallowing as much as I can to stop the void from
growing
To end this constant vacancy of emotions
To feel something, finally
But what

Crumbling Down

My smile will fade today
Only to return on a sunnier day

My mouth will be quiet
My voice soft
Only to speak when spoken to

My eyes want to remain closed
To see nothing of what it accepts to be true

My joints shake with uncertainty
Only to amplify the unrest within

You can see me now as a house
The lights are on but there's no one home

I'm taking a vacation from myself
Leaving only my body behind
Emotionally void
Nothing to hear but static
A deathly white noise

The Haunting

Nostalgia creeps in
Everytime I feel a certain way
It's always a revolving door

My mind
Endless visions of the past
Things that bring me comfort
No one can tell me I'm wrong

When I put you on
To me you are a masterpiece
A memory shared with my parents
With a tuna fish sandwich in hand
You come around the corner from the computer
room

How do I wish to hear and see you again
Why must I have another grave dug in my mind
So I'll sit back and press play

Watch the recording playout
A vision of us
Together forever
Until my time is up

Don't Be Foolish

For what I have
Is not for you to know
I will not sell myself
To be recognized
To be scrutinized
No one to call a friend

You speak of many triggers
Boldly, you all reveal your insecurities
But there is no evidence of mental instabilities
Leaving no room for real empathy
Just annoyance

I hold back from releasing my genetic defect
Knowing there wouldn't be sympathy for me
They are too young to know the ravages of war
The mental disease that continues to destroy every
last part of me

To think they are immaculate is false
To underestimate them is foolish
So I keep my mouth closed

Not wanting to share
The blood soaked history of my diseased mind

Is This For Real

Imagine if this was all just a dream
You weren't really gone
We were all just in a corona haze
Bodies blazing
Reality lucid
Should we even say goodbye

What happens
If I don't want to accept this reality
You are still in the ICU
You'd be coming home in a few months
We visit you
Moments of encouragement
Pure love

Your last call, still haunts me
I said nothing
You struggling for air
Telling us "I love you all"
Your final goodbye
The last time we heard your voice
I did not know what was to come

Midnight Stroll

Winds blow steadily tonight
The stars are bright
Distant
The moon sparkles
Spotlighting the insecurities
I keep deep inside

The walk is long
As it should be
The eeriness is not foreign
It's home
Because I am alone most of the time
I wouldn't call it a friend
It was once my greatest enemy

I have not cried since he passed
Cannot see myself having typical emotions
Emotions which are biologically linked
Most trauma has been repaired

I don't want to sound insensitive or seem inhuman
I miss him like the rest of them

Only good things and calm
Come from the memories I cherish most
From the beginning to the sudden end

It's getting chilly again
This can't be another upset
Could it be grief
I don't know
All I need to do is keep walking
Make it home
One foot in front of the other
They are waiting for me
I am waiting for the end

The Golden Gate

Flowers have bloomed
The air perfumed
Birds whistling all around
The sun, it shines
On me, for the first time
Without any feeling of anxiety

I walk through the garden
Look at the fountains
To find that I wasn't always alone
Just outside, the golden gate
My family happily awaits

Within my hand
I hold the key to that gate
And for the first time
I unlock the gate
Love rushes in
I just can't wait

Maybe Not A Poem

I know this is naughty of me
There is one thing I want people to have
A false sense of security
To rely on me
When I'm at my most unreliable

They make me feel like an object
Whose purpose is to make certain
They are loved above all
To confirm their actions are better than my own

I don't understand what this younger generation's
deal is
They need to be loved by all
They are unique
Even though their motives are shared
Life is not a popularity contest

I never go out of my way
To make myself loved by anyone
Or try to confirm my actions are good
If you are going to be unique

Try less
Let your light shine
Be Blessed

Where Is God

I've traveled so far
To come to the very edge
Not to look down
But to look up
To gaze at the stars
The cosmos
Trying to understand God's will
His plan for me
And for this wretched place called Earth
I cannot say I don't know him
I've spat in his face more than once
Cursed his name for what went wrong
Now at the edge
I look up
To see his designs
Which are greater than me

Denouement

To Believe

Oh Mary
How I needed you then
When I prayed to you
All of my heart
All of my soul
Poured into each word

"Hail, Mary"
"The Lord is with thee"
"Blessed art thou"

I envisioned myself
Weeping in your robes
Hiding behind your veil
To shut out the world I had to face
Seek shelter from my own mind

Crying on the floor
Fetal position
Hoping
Praying
That my life would end

I saw no hope

There was only one option

People have no idea about my life

How I hid behind your veil

Praying to you

To plead to God

For clarity

To know I do belong somewhere in the world

Just Let Me Know

Record after record
Lyric to lyric
You are present
Guiding me
Navigating my light
Your hand on my shoulder
"Things come in time"
"Be patient, my son"

Holding on to each note
Clutching onto each climax
My soul just wants to crescendo
Leaving behind existence
Life is not worth living without you
I no longer have innocence
I see through adult eyes
But cry like a child

Will you let me know
When I'm getting closer to the design
To the moment when the light is strongest
Don't want to let you down

I'm only human
I'll fall
Make mistakes
Just let me know

Record to record
Lyric to lyric
I can find you within me
Igniting my fire
The passion you had
When your records played

About the Author

Jimmy Cullen is a dedicated barista with the intention to be understood by the world. Born in New York but raised in New Jersey, Jimmy has battled with mental illness all his life. He was officially diagnosed with Bipolar I after his suicide attempt. Since then he's been holding on to a steady job while trying to find the best avenue to express himself emotionally. Poetry has become his vehicle for navigating through tough waters and finding moments of enlightenment. Jimmy looks forward to expressing himself to you. All you have to do is listen.

A Note to our Furious Readers

From all of us at Read Furiously, we hope you enjoyed our latest installment in our One 'n Done series, *Showboi: Too Deep Too Care.*

There are countless narratives in this world and we would like to share as many of them as possible with our Furious Readers.

It is with this in mind that we pledge to donate a portion of these book sales to causes that are special to Read Furiously. These causes are chosen with the intent to better the lives of others who are struggling to tell their own stories.

Reading is more than a passive activity – it is the opportunity to play an active role within our world. The causes we support are culturally and socially conscious to encourage a sense of civic responsibility associated with the act of reading. Each cause has been researched thoroughly, discussed openly, and voted upon carefully by our team of Read Furiously editors.

To find out more about who, what, why, and where Read Furiously lends its support, please visit our website at readfuriously.com/charity

Happy reading and giving, Furious Readers!

Read Often, Read Well,
Read Furiously!

More in the One 'n Done Series

What About Tuesday
Adam Wilson
978-0-9965227-9-3

Brethren Hollow
Bill Hemmig
978-1-7337360-8-4

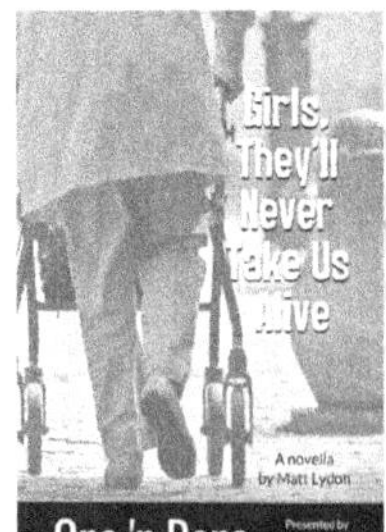

Gurls, They'll Never Take Us Alive
Matt Lydon
978-1-7337360-3-9

Helium
Adam Wilson
and Jeff Chin
978-1-7337360-5-3

The Legend of Dave Bradley
S Atzeni
978-1-7371758-8-9

The Path Home
A.J. Pelligrino
979-8-9868097-8-6

Brooklyn Family Album
Margaret Montet
Coming 2024

The Cursed Sailor and the Golden Conch
GR Lear
979-8-9868097-6-2

Showboi: Too Deep Too Care
Jimmy Cullen
979-8-9868097-6-2

Wund to Space
Rowan Kilduf
Coming 2024

Find the whole series at readfuriously.com/one

www.ingramcontent.com/pod-product-compliance
Lightning Source LLC
Chambersburg PA
CBHW060507300726
48975CB00008B/2683